The 1968 Democratic Convention

SECOND SERIES

Tom McGowen

Children's Press®
A Division of Scholastic Inc.
New York • Toronto • London • Auckland • Sydney
Mexico City • New Delhi • Hong Kong
Danbury, Connecticut

Photographs © 2003: AP/Wide World Photos: 15 (Hong Seong-Chan), 21, 39 bottom; Corbis Images/Bettmann: cover bottom, 39 top; Getty Images: 27 (Neil Jacobs), cover top; Hulton|Archive/Getty Images: 19, 41; Magnum Photos: 31 (Bob Adelman), 3, 45 top left (Raymond Depardon), 32 (Paul Fusco), 22, 30, 35 (Burt Glinn), 11, 16, 18, 44 top (Philip Jones Griffiths), 29, 44 bottom right (Erich Hartmann), 26, 38, 45 bottom (Hiroji Kubota), 5, 6, 13, 37, 44 bottom left, 45 top right (Roger Malloch), 28 (Inge Morath); Stockphoto.com/Charles Moore: 25; The Image Works/Topham: 36.

Library of Congress Cataloging-in-Publication Data
McGowen, Tom.
  The 1968 Democratic Convention / Tom McGowen.
    p. cm. — (Cornerstones of freedom. Second series)
  Summary: Presents background information on the cold war and the Vietnam war as context for events of the Democratic Party Convention of 1968 in Chicago, Illinois, focusing on the street confrontations between police and activists during the convention.
  Includes bibliographical references and index.
    ISBN 0-516-24220-2
    1. Democratic National Convention (1968: Chicago, Ill.)—Juvenile literature. 2. United States—Politics and government—1963–1969—Juvenile literature. [1. Democratic National Convention (1968: Chicago, Ill.) 2. United States—Politics and government—1963–1969. 3. Political conventions.] I. Title. II. Series: Cornerstones of freedom. Second series.
JK23131968 .M39 2003
324.2736—dc21

                                        2003005662

CHILDREN'S PRESS, and CORNERSTONES OF FREEDOM™, and associated logos are trademarks and or registered trademarks of Scholastic Library Publishing. SCHOLASTIC and associated logos are trademarks and or registered trademarks of Scholastic Inc.

1 2 3 4 5 6 7 8 9 10 R 12 11 10 09 08 07 06 05 04 03

THE WHOLE WORLD IS WATCHING! Inside the convention center, the politicians were trying to go about their business. It was late August, 1968. They had come to Chicago, Illinois, the nation's second-largest city, to hold the Democratic Party's National Convention. Such conventions were held every four years. Representatives (called **delegates**) of the party from every state in the country came together for the purpose of picking the party's candidate for president and deciding what the party's positions should be on the most important issues of the day.

★ ★ ★ ★

Democratic conventions were famous for often being rowdy affairs, but no one had ever seen anything quite like this. The convention seemed to be taking place in two separate locations. One was inside the convention center, where the politicians were making speeches, the delegates were meeting and casting votes, and reporters from newspapers, magazines, and television stations were trying to explain it all for their readers and viewers.

The "other" convention was taking place outside, on the streets and in the parks of Chicago. There, thousands of another kind of delegate had gathered. They represented not a traditional political party but those many Americans who had come to believe that the major political parties—the Democrats and the Republicans—did not truly represent them.

These individuals, most of them young, believed that the major political parties were not really addressing the most important issues of the day, especially the United States' involvement in the war in Vietnam. Knowing that the country's media would be focused on the convention, they had come to Chicago to protest and to demonstrate, to meet, to rally, and to march. Most of all, they wanted to draw attention to themselves. They intended to make the media, and the politicians inside, and the millions of Americans watching at home, take notice of them and the causes they were so passionate about.

Separating the two conventions were police—huge numbers of them—and soldiers. As the politicians went about their business inside the convention center, the

Police move in on demonstrators in Grant Park. Many Americans saw demonstrators and activists as a threat to law and order, but a government commission determined that the violence in Chicago was the result of a "police riot."

protestors went about their activities outside, and they clashed again and again with the police and soldiers who had been called out to "keep the peace." Arrests and beatings took place. The police and soldiers used so much

During World War II, two fingers raised in the air like this was understood to mean "V for victory," but in the 1960s, opponents of the Vietnam War, like these demonstrators in Chicago during the 1968 Democratic Convention, adopted the gesture as the "peace sign."

tear gas that delegates and candidates for office could smell it all the way up on the top floors of the towering luxury hotels where they were staying for the convention.

Inside, the politicians began to argue among themselves. Already deeply divided on many issues, they now began to differ about what was going on in the streets. At home, Americans read the newspapers and watched the events on television and wondered what was happening to the country. Some worried that the United States was on the verge of a revolution or a civil war. In the streets of Chicago, the protestors readied themselves for the next clash with the police and sent up a chant that could be heard even inside the convention center. "The whole world is watching!" they chanted again and again. "The whole world is watching! The whole world is watching!" Even those who disagreed on the issues of the day agreed that the demonstrators were right about this.

A TROUBLED YEAR

In many ways, the disturbances in Chicago in August 1968 did not come as a great surprise to most Americans. By the time the Democrats held their annual convention, 1968 had already been one of the most troubled years in American history. Many historians and journalists believed the country had not been so divided since the Civil War, more than 100 years earlier. With U.S. troops fighting in the southeast Asian nation of Vietnam, and so much unrest within the United States, it felt to many Americans that the country was at war both overseas and at home.

VIETNAM

What had made 1968 so troubled? By 1968, the U.S. involvement in the war in Vietnam had reached its greatest point, in terms of the numbers of soldiers sent to fight, the amount and kinds of weapons sent to fight the war with, and U.S. bombing raids on targets in Vietnam. As U.S. involvement had steadily increased, or escalated, since the early 1960s, so had the level of opposition to the war within the United States.

That opposition was growing for several reasons. Since the early 1960s, government officials in the administrations of presidents John F. Kennedy, who served as president from 1961 until his death in 1963, and Lyndon B. Johnson, who became president when Kennedy was assassinated and still held office in 1968, had been promising Americans that although U.S. involvement in Vietnam was necessary, it would be brief and limited.

By 1968, it had become clear that this would not be the case. At the end of 1963, there had been almost 17,000 U.S. troops in Vietnam. By the end of 1965, there were almost 125,000 young American men in combat in that country. By the end of 1967, that number had risen to 500,000, a figure that seemed unimaginable when President Kennedy had first announced, early in his administration, that he was sending a handful of military "advisors" to Vietnam. As the number of U.S. troops involved in the fighting rose, so did the number of Americans killed or wounded in combat.

TET

With each increase in U.S. involvement in Vietnam, the government promised the American people its goals in the war were being reached. Victory was near, Americans were assured, there was "light at the end of the tunnel."

Up until 1968, a majority of Americans believed the government's claims that the war was going according to plan. That changed considerably in the first month of 1968.

* * * *

For the Vietnamese, January 1968 coincided with their annual festival of Tet Nguyen Dan, usually referred to as Tet for short. Tet is the Vietnamese celebration of the lunar new year. In Vietnamese culture, the celebration also marks the beginning of spring. Tet is a time for new beginnings, the exchange of gifts and best wishes, and family reunions. During the days of Tet, an individual's actions are considered especially important. The Vietnamese believe that the way one acts during Tet helps determine the way the rest of the year will go.

THE VIETNAM WAR: BACKGROUND

In 1968, Tet certainly marked a "new beginning" for the Vietnam War. In that struggle, the United States was providing military aid to the government of South Vietnam, which was fighting a war against communist **guerrillas**, known as the Vietcong, and the army of North Vietnam.

Vietnam had been at war for many years. Since 1861, all or part of Vietnam, along with the neighboring countries of Laos and Cambodia, had been a colony of France. During World War II, Japan took control of Vietnam from France, but when the war ended with Japan's defeat, the French returned.

By now, though, the Vietnamese were demanding their independence, and they began to actively resist French rule. The most important leader in that struggle was Ho Chi Minh,

HO CHI MINH

To many Americans, Ho Chi Minh was a symbol of communist aggression, but his own people remember him as the father of Vietnamese independence. Born in rural Vietnam in 1890 and educated as a young man in France, Ho saw guerrilla warfare as the way for Vietnam to win its independence. He was certain that the Vietnamese could outlast any foreign power in their country. "You can kill 10 of my men for every one I kill of yours," he told the French and later the Americans, "yet even at those odds, you will lose and I will win." Six years after his death in 1975, Ho was proved right.

the founder of the Vietnamese communist party. With the departure of the Japanese in 1945, Ho Chi Minh declared Vietnam independent, using some of the words from the American Declaration of Independence. He even asked for U.S. help.

France was determined to keep control of Vietnam, however, and war between the French and the Vietnamese opposition, who were known as the Vietminh, began in 1946. The war lasted for the next eight years, with French control strongest in Vietnamese cities in the South and the Vietminh strongest in rural areas in the North.

In 1954, Vietnamese forces led by the soon-to-be legendary general Vo Nguyen Giap surrounded and then overran a heavily fortified French base at a place called Dien Bien Phu. The shocking defeat convinced the French to give up their control of Vietnam.

In the negotiations that ended the war with France, Vietnam was divided into two countries, North Vietnam and South Vietnam. For the most part, the Vietminh and their supporters held the North, while those still sympathetic to France or opposed to the Vietminh held the South. The division of Vietnam was supposed to be temporary. National elections were to be held in 1956 to unite the North and the South. It was widely expected that Ho Chi Minh, the most popular leader in Vietnam, would win the election.

"It became necessary to destroy it in order to save it," was what one U.S. officer said about the destruction in South Vietnam caused by U.S. efforts to repel the Tet offensive. Here, a South Vietnamese refugee woman makes her way with her remaining possessions through a U.S. military patrol in a section of Saigon destroyed by American artillery and helicopter fire.

The elections were never held. Eager to extend its influence in Southeast Asia after defeating Japan in World War II, the United States slowly began to replace the French by supporting and providing aid to the government in South Vietnam. At the time, the United States was becoming more heavily engaged every day in what is known as the Cold War—the struggle with the Communist state of the Soviet Union for political and economic power and influence around the globe. Vietnam quickly became one of the Cold War's testing grounds.

The United States was unwilling to risk that Ho Chi Minh, a Communist, might become the legitimate leader of a united Vietnam. With the support of the U.S., the government in South Vietnam refused to hold the promised national elections. Vietnam now seemed to be permanently divided between North and South.

By the late 1950s, however, many Vietnamese in South Vietnam were rebelling against the government there. They wanted a united Vietnam, free of foreign influence, and they naturally looked to the North, where Ho Chi Minh had built an independent communist state, for help and inspiration. These rebels became known in the United States as the Vietcong, for Vietnamese Communists.

With help from North Vietnam, by the 1960s the Vietcong were winning increasing political support and military success in the South. Determined to support the government of South Vietnam, the United States committed an ever greater amount of military support, in the form of soldiers and equipment, to fighting the Vietcong and their North Vietnamese allies.

THE DEATH OF DIEM

Ngo Dinh Diem became the first prime minister of South Vietnam in 1954. With U.S. support, he cancelled the national elections scheduled for 1956. Over the next several years, many elements in South Vietnam began to oppose his rule, especially those who wanted a united Vietnam free of American influence. By 1963, with much of his country in rebellion, Diem began to hint that he might negotiate with his opponents and the North Vietnamese. The U.S. then launched a plan to have Diem's generals overthrow him, which resulted in his assassination.

By 1968, that support had taken the form of more than 500,000 troops, billions of dollars, and an increasingly ferocious war that included the U.S. bombing of North Vietnamese cities and civilian targets. Each year, the number of American troops, and U.S. casualties, in Vietnam rose. Unlike today, when service in the United States is purely voluntary, the government of the United States obtained troops through what was known as the **selective service**, or **draft**. At age 18,

THE GULF OF TONKIN RESOLUTION

As was true in Korea in the early 1950s, the U.S. military action was conducted without an official declaration of war by Congress. In 1965, following an alleged North Vietnamese attack on U.S. naval vessels in the Gulf of Tonkin, President Johnson asked Congress for unlimited authority to conduct the war as he saw fit. The resulting Gulf of Tonkin Resolution, which gave Johnson the authority he asked for, passed the Senate by a vote of 98 to 2.

Burning one's draft card, as this demonstrator in Chicago in August 1968 is doing, was a popular—and illegal—method of showing one's opposition to the Vietnam War.

★ ★ ★ ★

young men had to register for the selective service. If selected, or drafted, by the government, they then had to provide two years of mandatory military service, some of it, possibly, in Vietnam.

THE TET OFFENSIVE

All the while, Americans were assured by their government that the United States was close to achieving its goals in Vietnam. With the arrival of Tet in January 1968 seemed to come proof that this was not the case.

January 31st on the American calendar marked the arrival of the first day of Tet on the Vietnamese calendar. Masterminded by General Giap, the North Vietnamese Army (NVA) and the Vietcong (VC) had prepared a new year's surprise for the U.S. and South Vietnamese forces.

By that date, tens of thousands of NVA and VC troops had surrounded and were besieging Khe Sanh, an isolated Marine garrison in northwest South Vietnam. The situation led to fears that Khe Sanh would become another Dien Bien Phu.

With attention focused on Khe Sanh, NVA and VC forces infiltrated the South. Early on the morning of January 31, they attacked virtually every major city and town of South Vietnam, as well as most U.S. air and military bases. They took control of the ancient Vietnamese capital city of Hue and of large sections of the modern capital of Saigon, even briefly overrunning the U.S. embassy there.

Dead comrades beside them, U.S. military police take cover inside the compound of the U.S. embassy in Saigon as it comes under attack on the first day of the Tet offensive, January 31, 1968.

Besieged U.S. soldiers fire from a building in the South Vietnamese capital city of Saigon during the Tet offensive. Images like these, from what was supposed to be the U.S. stronghold in Vietnam, stunned many Americans, who believed that the United States was winning the war.

BACK HOME

Vietnam was the first war that Americans could watch regular footage from on their television news. The first success of the Tet offensive made for shocking viewing. For many Americans, whether they had been opposed to the war before this or not, it now seemed that something was dreadfully wrong.

For them, it seemed the government must have been either dishonest or incompetent when it claimed the war was going according to plan. Earlier that very same month, Johnson had assured them in a speech that the U.S. forces and their South Vietnamese allies were in control of 65 percent of South Vietnam and that total victory was near. Now they had been shown that rather than approaching victory, the United States was, in fact, in very little control of any part of South Vietnam.

Among those who were stunned by the Tet offensive was the president of the United States, Lyndon B. Johnson (LBJ). Since 1963, Johnson had steadily increased the number of U.S. arms and troops in Vietnam, relying on the information of his advisors and their assurances that the United States was winning.

Now, Tet had shown him how disastrously wrong this advice had been. Within days of the offensive, the commander of the U.S. military forces in Vietnam, General William Westmoreland, asked Johnson for more than 200,000 new troops. When Johnson presented the request

A U.S. soldier scrambles for cover in Saigon during the Tet offensive. The Vietcong guerrillas were supposed to be strongest in the countryside; their willingness to mount direct attacks in South Vietnam's cities surprised U.S. military planners.

to his top advisors on the war, they told him that more troops would not help. Not only was the war not going according to plan, they told the president, it was, in fact, unwinnable.

A CHANGING SOCIETY

Even before Tet, the Vietnam War had already cost Johnson a great deal of his popularity. After becoming president on the death of John Kennedy in November 1963, Johnson had been elected on his own in 1964 with one of the largest majorities in U.S. history. He began his first term promising to create what he called "the Great Society" through the establishment of ambitious government programs covering everything from civil rights for African Americans and other minorities to a "war on poverty" and better medical care for poor and elderly citizens.

With a presidential election scheduled for November 1968, Johnson found himself in a very difficult political position. His own political party, the Democrats, were split on the war, with the party's **liberal** wing generally in support

A weary and haggard President Lyndon Johnson (center) confers with Secretary of State Dean Rusk (left) and Secretary of Defense Robert McNamara (right). These top advisors to Johnson were considered two of the primary architects of the Vietnam War, but by early 1968 even their confidence was rapidly fading.

of finding a way to end the war, while other Democrats continued to support Johnson on Vietnam. Meanwhile, the war was costing billions of dollars, leaving the country with less to spend on Johnson's Great Society programs.

At the same time, the Great Society was becoming almost as divisive as the war. In 1964, Johnson and the Democrats had trounced the Republicans in the national election, in large part because the Democrats were seen as being more liberal on the kinds of issues the Great Society addressed, especially **civil rights**.

But by 1968, the Republicans were gaining in strength. Rather than opposing the war, many Americans believed Johnson had not been aggressive enough in directing it. Many of those who favored the war looked to the Republican party for leadership.

In addition, many Americans had begun to oppose many of Johnson's civil rights programs. The civil rights movement had evolved from focusing on an end to legal **segregation** in the South to a broader challenge to other aspects of American society, including an end to poverty and to the war in Vietnam. In fact, the movement's most influential leader, Martin Luther King, Jr., had specifically called opposition to the Vietnam War a civil rights issue.

The logic of such an idea was presented most famously by the heavyweight boxing champion of the world, Muhammad Ali, an outspoken African American who was already controversial for his friendship with the black **radical** Malcolm X and his membership in the **Black Muslims**. When Ali was drafted in 1967, he refused to be inducted into the military,

As a gesture of protest against the way African Americans were treated in the United States, the Olympic sprinters Tommie Smith (center) and John Carlos (right) gave the "black power" salute after being presented with the gold and silver medals in the 200-meter race at the 1968 Olympic Games in Mexico City. Because of their gesture, the two runners were thrown off the U.S. Olympic team and had their medals taken from them.

Following the rioting that occurred in early April 1968 upon the news that the civil rights leader Martin Luther King, Jr., had been assassinated, debris and wreckage in the streets of Washington, D.C., reflect the anger and confusion felt there and across the country.

risking jail and causing his championship title to be taken away from him. "I got no quarrel with them Vietcong," Ali said when asked to explain his actions.

While King had stressed nonviolence and **integration**, a new, more outspoken, more aggressive generation of civil rights **activists** was now calling for "black power." They urged using "any means necessary," including violence, to gain what they wanted.

As a result of their activities, violence began to flare in many places throughout the United States. Beginning in the summer of 1965, and continuing for four "long, hot summers," violent riots occurred in the black ghettos of many of the nation's largest cities, most notably Los Angeles, California; Newark, New Jersey; and Detroit, Michigan. Troops had to be called in to end the burning, looting, and sniping. On their evening news telecasts, Americans could now see tanks rumbling through the streets of their own cities, not just in faraway places like Saigon and Hue.

The response by many whites was a **backlash** against the civil rights movement. The movement had gone "too far," such citizens believed; the government had done all it could do, and the response was violent ingratitude in the form of rioting and calls for black power.

American society, these citizens believed, was becoming increasingly out of control. In addition to the urban violence in the black ghettos, there were the increasingly numerous public protests and demonstrations against the war in Vietnam. That many of the protesters were young college students only seemed to make matters worse to those who supported

the war. To such people, these students seemed ungrateful and unpatriotic, unaware of the privileges they enjoyed by virtue of being Americans. To hear demonstrators at antiwar rallies chant such slogans as, "Hey, hey LBJ, how many kids did you kill today?" or "Ho, Ho, Ho Chi Minh, Hanoi's going to win" seemed to these Americans to be a kind of treason.

The "generation gap" then coming into play in American society only seemed to add to such differences. Following World War II, the country had enjoyed a period of great economic prosperity, accompanied by a "baby boom," or increase in the number of children being born. With the country prosperous and at peace, people felt confident about raising large families.

By the 1960s, these "baby boomers" were entering their teens. Quite simply, the country was becoming younger, in that society consisted of a much greater number of young people. The resulting "youth culture" or "counter-culture" was changing the country in a way that their parents and grandparents sometimes found difficult to understand or accept. Rock 'n roll now ruled the airwaves and record charts, pushing older forms of music aside. New fashions came to the forefront, with youngsters rejecting the business suits, hats, and short hair of their dads and the practical dresses and ornate hairdos of their moms. The young favored casual dress, especially blue jeans, and long, often unkempt hair. Other kinds of behavior seemed to be changing as well, with many of the young willing to engage in drug use and sexual behavior that to the older generations seemed disturbingly casual, immoral, and even dangerous. Many

of these young people called themselves "hippies," from
the slang word "hip," meaning well-informed about important things.

THE FALL OF A PRESIDENT

All these changes left President Johnson in a very difficult position. Those voters who feared that America was falling into chaos were calling for "law and order." In general, they were turning to the Republicans or the most conservative wing of the Democratic party. Unable to find a solution to the mounting crisis in Vietnam, Johnson was

Police hold back demonstrators at a George Wallace campaign appearance at Wrigley Field in Chicago in 1968. The Democrats were stunned at the level of support that Wallace, an anti-civil rights southerner, drew in the North. To the Republicans, Wallace's appeal suggested that the Democrats were vulnerable in the 1968 presidential election.

trapped, for those who were most likely to support his Great Society programs were also those most likely to oppose the war.

Even before the shock of the Tet offensive, the Democrats were dividing over the war. In late 1967, many liberal Democrats were looking for a anti-war candidate to oppose Johnson for the party's presidential nomination the following year. The search was led by a young congressman from New York named Allard Lowenstein.

Few Democrats wanted to challenge a president from their own party. Even with opposition to the war increasing, most people believed that Johnson was unbeatable in 1968.

Robert Kennedy, the younger brother of former president John Kennedy, was the first choice of Lowenstein and most of Johnson's opponents within the party. The former attorney general of the United States and now a senator from New York, Kennedy was in some ways the ideal candidate, a charismatic liberal supporter of civil rights and an increasingly outspoken opponent of the war. He was also known to be not particularly fond of Johnson.

Like Eugene McCarthy, Senator Robert Kennedy appealed to the hopes and idealism of young Americans. Kennedy had much more support than McCarthy among the poor and minority groups.

27

Eugene McCarthy addresses a campaign rally at Madison Square Garden in New York City during his 1968 presidential campaign. McCarthy was generally known more for his intelligence than his charisma, but his appeal to the young in 1968 led journalists to refer to him as "the Pied Piper."

★ ★ ★ ★

But Kennedy was not willing to take on the president, and he turned Lowenstein down. Lowenstein and others then tried several others before Senator Eugene McCarthy of Minnesota, a former professional baseball player, college professor, and published poet who had been one of the first members of Congress to turn against the war, accepted the challenge. On November 30, 1967, McCarthy announced that he would challenge Johnson in the Democratic party primaries in early 1968. His sole issue was to be opposition to the war.

Few thought that the intellectual McCarthy would pose a serious challenge to Johnson. Most expected little more from him than an honorable moral crusade. McCarthy himself admitted on several occasions that he really wasn't sure he even wanted to be president. The young antiwar hippies, however, were thrilled to have a candidate other than Johnson, and they flocked to the state of New Hampshire, the traditional site of the first presidential primary. There, they vowed to "get clean for Gene"—cut and comb their hair, trim their beards and mustaches, and put on nice, clean clothes so as not to alienate New Hampshire voters.

On March 12, 1968, Americans learned that the Tet Offensive and discontent over the direction of the war and U.S. society had damaged Johnson far more than anyone had imagined. Expected to win a landslide victory, Johnson beat McCarthy by only seven percentage points in the New Hampshire Democratic primary, a shocking result. More shocking still was that McCarthy won 20 of the state's 24 delegates to the party's national convention, to be held in August 1968.

Bigger shocks were ahead. Four days after the New Hampshire primary, Robert Kennedy announced that he would, in fact, now seek the Democratic nomination for president. Just more than two weeks later, on March 31, Johnson announced in a nationwide broadcast that he would not run for reelection in 1968. It was the first time in the nation's history that a president, who under the Constitution is also the commander-in-chief of the armed forces, had voluntarily given up his office with the country at war.

In Washington, D.C., on March 16, 1968, Robert Kennedy announces that he will run for the Democratic nomination for president. "I run to seek new policies," Kennedy said that day, "policies to end the bloodshed in Vietnam and in our cities, policies to close the gaps that now exist between black and white, between rich and poor, between young and old, in this country and around the world."

National Guardsmen stand guard as firefighters do their work on a burned-out block of 14th Street in Washington, D.C., during the rioting that followed the death of Martin Luther King, Jr.

THE LONGEST, HOTTEST SUMMER

Johnson was exhausted and depressed by his inability to find a solution in Vietnam and to bring about a greater unity in U.S. society. He recognized that he had become a symbol of the various divisions in the society, and he hoped that by removing himself from the political process these divisions would start to heal.

Instead, his announcement seemed to set off a powderkeg, and American society exploded. Less than one week later, on April 4, 1968, Martin Luther King, Jr., was assassinated in Memphis, Tennessee, by an escaped convict, drifter, and white supremacist named James Earl Ray. With news of his death, more than 100 cities erupted into rioting and flames. Chief among them was the nation's capital, Washington, D.C., where downtown blocks burned in sight of the White House, gunfire could be heard, and troops had to be called in. "This is astonishing," one television journalist reported from the streets of Washington. "This looks like something that could be happening in South Vietnam."

Several of Martin Luther King's closest aides mourn over his coffin at his funeral in Atlanta, Georgia, in April 1968.

For hundreds of miles between New York City and Washington, D.C., mourners lined the railroad tracks to pay their last respects as Robert Kennedy's funeral train rolled by in June 1968.

Meanwhile, the political process rolled on. Kennedy and McCarthy traded victories in various state primaries, while Hubert Humphrey, Johnson's vice-president, watched from Washington, hoping that in Chicago he would have enough votes from former Johnson loyalists to gain the nomination for himself.

By June, Kennedy's campaign was gaining momentum. Huge, almost frenzied crowds turned out wherever he appeared. Kennedy spoke, wrote one reporter, "for those who could not speak for themselves." He made appearances in places where few politicians ever went, such as the black ghettos of Gary, Indiana, and the Native American reservations of South Dakota. The Reverend Channing Phillips, a leader in the black community of Washington, D.C., said that Kennedy "had this fantastic ability to communicate hope to some pretty rejected people." Robert Kennedy, said the civil rights leader Charles Evers, "was the last white man in America who could bring peace between the races."

The sense of loss and tragedy was thus all the more devastating when Robert Kennedy, like his brother before him, was killed by an assassin. The murder took place on the night of June 4, in Los Angeles, just after Kennedy had thanked his supporters and claimed victory in the California primary. His victory, many political experts thought, had made him the favorite to win the Democratic nomination for president. More than a million people lined the railroad tracks as a special train carried Kennedy's body from New York City, where his funeral was held, to Washington, D.C., where he was buried. A sense of fear and disbelief was felt across the country. What was happening to the United States? What would happen next?

THE BATTLE OF MICHIGAN AVENUE

And so they all came to Chicago in late August of 1968, that most troubled of American years. The Democrats

THE BEATS

The presence of Allen Ginsberg, one of the country's most famous poets, in Chicago during the Democratic National Convention was highly symbolic. With the novelists Jack Kerouac and William Burroughs (who was also in Chicago), Ginsberg was the leading member of the literary group known as the Beat Generation, or, simply, the Beats. The Beats became famous in the mid-1950s, when their innovative literary works and unconventional lifestyle, both of which challenged mainstream American society, alarmed and excited many Americans. Many regarded the Beats as the true ancestors of the hippies and activists who gathered in Chicago.

★　★　★　★

came, hoping to repair their fractured party and to select a presidential candidate that would allow them to hold on to political power at the national level. The demonstrators and the protesters and the young came, too, as individuals and as members of various groups, such as the Yippies (the Youth International Party), the SDS (Students for a Democratic Society), the Mobe (the National Mobilization to End the War in Vietnam), SNCC (Student Non-violent Coordinating Committee), and others. They had been planning since the previous year to meet in Chicago, where they hoped to be allowed to camp in the city's parks and mount several days of protests against the war.

The media came, too, of course, broadcast journalists and cameramen, and newspaper and magazine reporters, and famous writers and musicians, too, such as novelist Norman Mailer, poet Allen Ginsberg, the French man of letters Jean Genet, folk singer Phil Ochs, and the radical rock group MC5. With the media came the eyes of America, and indeed, the eyes of the world, watching events unfold on television and newspapers and magazines. There was truth in the words the protesters chanted; the whole world was watching, or so it seemed.

Waiting for all these different groups and individuals in Chicago was that city's mayor, Richard Daley. It was said of Daley that next to President Johnson, he was the country's most powerful Democrat. A supporter of Johnson first and

The mayor of Chicago, Richard Daley, waves his fist from the floor of the convention. Daley's power in Chicago was so great that he was referred to simply as "the Boss."

now of Humphrey, Daley was among those Democrats who believed that the voices of protest and dissent had grown much too loud and unruly. After the rioting in Chicago that followed the death of Martin Luther King, Daley had criticized the city's police commissioner for being too gentle with the rioters. The police, Daley said, should have been ordered to "shoot to kill" rioters.

For the convention, he intended to present Chicago to the rest of the nation as a showcase for "law and order." The Democrats and demonstrators thus arrived to find Chicago

35

Barbed-wire cages protected the jeeps driven by the soldiers called out by Mayor Daley to "defend" Chicago against what he called "unruly protesters." Daley had assembled a force of 7,500 U.S. regular army troops, 6,000 National Guardsmen, and 12,000 policemen to secure his city.

an armed city, patrolled not just by police in full riot gear but by more than 6,000 National Guardsmen and an even greater number of regular army troops, many armed with machine guns and rocket launchers. Their windshields wrapped in barbed wire, army jeeps patrolled the streets and the parks where the young planned to gather.

The Democratic Convention officially began on Monday, August 26. By that time, there had already been two nights of clashes between the demonstrators and the police and the soldiers. Denied permits to sleep in the city's parks, the demonstrators were forced out each night at 11 P.M., often with billy clubs and tear gas. The demonstrators were confrontational but largely nonviolent; the police and national guardsmen confrontational and violent.

★ ★ ★ ★

For several nights, while the Democrats met inside the convention hall, the demonstrators and law enforcement officials engaged in a series of confrontations in the streets and parks of Chicago. In one famous incident, hundreds of demonstrators, dozens of reporters, and even some uninvolved Chicago residents were injured by police billy clubs and tear gas. Dozens of demonstrators were pushed by a line of charging police through a huge plate glass window in the front of a Chicago restaurant. This was called the Battle of Michigan Avenue by Chicago newspapers, after the street where it took place, one of Chicago's main thoroughfares.

Wielding billy clubs, police move in on demonstrators in Chicago's Grant Park during the 1968 Democratic National Convention.

Inside the convention center, the Democrats went about their business. A proposal for a "peace plank" in the party **platform** calling for an end to the Vietnam War was easily defeated. Although he had entered none of the state primaries, Hubert Humphrey was nominated for president on the first ballot. With the smell of tear gas drifting inside the convention senator, Senator Abraham Ribicoff of Connecticut, while speaking in favor of the peace **plank**, denounced what he called "**Gestapo** tactics on the streets of Chicago."

Television cameras then captured Mayor Daley gesturing angrily at Ribicoff and shouting at him.

THE CENTER CANNOT HOLD

The two gatherings in Chicago ended with the Democrats, and the country, also, no less divided than before. Though many Americans blamed the demonstrators for the unrest in Chicago, a government commission appointed to examine the violence concluded that the Battle of Michigan Avenue was a "police riot." The so-called Chicago 7, leaders of the various groups that planned the demonstrations, were arrested and tried for numerous alleged felonies, including incitement to riot, but none were convicted of any serious charges.

Against the background of his own smiling face, the "Happy Warrior," Hubert Humphrey, accepts the nomination of the Democratic party as its candidate for president of the United States in 1968.

Delegates to the Paris peace talks on the Vietnam War wait to take their places around the table in May 1968. The conference's beginning was delayed for weeks when the representatives were unable to agree on the proper shape of the table.

Energized by the divisions among the Democrats and the country as a whole, the Republicans nominated Richard Nixon, former vice-president and congressman from California, as their candidate for president. Nixon campaigned on "law and order" and the promise that he had a "secret plan" to end the war, one that he could not, however, reveal details about until, and if, he was elected president.

In the meantime, Johnson, in the remaining months of his term, had agreed to open peace talks with the Vietnamese. Fearing that a peace agreement would doom his campaign, Nixon had a secret message relayed to the Vietnamese delegates to the talks. The message informed the Vietnamese that they should reject any and all peace terms until after the U.S. presidential election. Once safely elected, Nixon secretly told them, he would give them better terms.

Presidential candidate George Wallace blows a kiss to antiwar demonstrators at a campaign appearance in Baltimore, Maryland, in 1968. Formerly a Democrat and governor of Alabama, where he had vowed to uphold "segregation forever," Wallace ran as a third-party candidate for president in 1968, appealing to "law and order" Democrats.

39

★ ★ ★ ★

Loyal to Johnson until the end, Humphrey did not speak out against the war until just one week before the election. By that time, it was too late, and Richard Nixon was elected president by a very slim margin.

Once in office, Nixon revealed his secret plan. While reducing the number of American troops in Vietnam, he raised the level of bombing to unprecedented levels. During his years as president, the United States dropped more bomb tonnage on Vietnam than all sides combined dropped in World War II. Nixon's intent, he revealed to his advisors, was to "bomb North Vietnam to the peace table" while making them fear that he might even be a "madman" willing to use nuclear weapons against them.

Less than one year into Nixon's administration, 250,000 antiwar demonstrators gathered in Washington. It was one of the largest protests in the country's history. At the same time, Nixon was escalating the war by secretly and unlawfully authorizing the bombing and invasion of Vietnam's neighbors, Cambodia and Laos.

Once revealed, the bombing and invasion of Cambodia led to the resignation of several of Nixon's top advisors, as well as to numerous antiwar protests around the country. At one of these, at Kent State University in Ohio, four unarmed demonstrators were shot to death by the National Guard.

Worried by what he perceived as **rampant** "disloyalty" in the country and even within his own administration, Nixon authorized illegal wiretaps and surveillance against several of his top advisers, as well as against top Democrats and scores of antiwar and civil rights activists. When these activities and his attempts at a cover-up were revealed, Nixon faced impeachment proceedings in Congress. Cited in the acts of impeachment is the secret bombing and invasion of Cambodia. Facing certain conviction, in August 1974 Nixon became the first and only American president to resign from office.

By that time, U.S. troops had been out of Vietnam for about a year, leaving the war to the South Vietnamese. On April 30, 1975, Saigon fell to the North Vietnamese, re-uniting Vietnam and ending the only war the United States has ever lost.

The things that happened during the 1968 Democratic Convention convinced many Americans that protest marches and demonstrations had to be put to a stop. For many others, the result of the convention destroyed all hope that the Vietnam War could be quickly ended, and that changes could be made to help civil rights, and end racism and inequality. These young Americans had dreamed of helping America, but now the dream was dead.

Bloodied and wounded by police, these antiwar activists still manage to flash the peace sign as they leave Grant Park at the end of the convention.

Glossary

activist—a person who uses action, such as protests, demonstrations, and even violence, to cause change

backlash—a reaction against something that is happening within a community or nation

Black Muslims—African Americans who belong to the Muslim religion

civil rights—the rights of American citizens as provided by the U.S. constitution

delegates—persons chosen to represent a group of people at a convention or similar meeting

draft—a process of selecting men to be taken into the Armed Forces, by means of a lottery

Gestapo—the security police of Nazi Germany, who used vicious, brutal methods to control the people

guerrillas—soldiers who do not belong to a regular army, but act on their own, making quick raids and attacks

integration—bringing separate races together in order
to form a united nation

liberal—a person who believes in making changes in law,
government, and society in hopes of helping the
majority of people

plank—a political party's statement about what it believes
must be done to handle a particular problem

platform—a political party's list of ideas for what should
be done to solve the nation's main problems

radical—a person who is in favor of extreme changes in
the government and society

rampant—strong and active

segregation—a policy of keeping different races of
people separate from each other

selective service—a law that allows the government to
select men for compulsory military service

Timeline: The 1968

1965

MARCH 8
The first U.S. combat troops land in South Vietnam.

APRIL 17
The first peace march, by 25,000 people demonstrating against the war in Vietnam, takes place in Washington, D.C.

NOVEMBER
Marches and demonstrations against the war become widespread throughout the United States.

1967

OCTOBER 21
100,000 activists march and demonstrate in Washington, D.C.

· · · · · · · · · ·

DECEMBER 31
The Youth International Party, or "Yippies," is created.

JANUARY 3
Senator Eugene McCarthy of Minnesota announces that he is running against President Johnson as a Democratic candidate for president, opposing the war.

1968

JANUARY 30
North Vietnamese forces launch major attacks in South Vietnam.

· · · · · · · · ·

MARCH 16
Senator Robert Kennedy of New York announces that he is running as a Democratic candidate for president.

MARCH 31
President Johnson announces he will not run for re-election.

Democratic Convention

AUGUST 25
The first clash between police and activists occurs in Chicago's Lincoln Park.

AUGUST 26
The Convention begins. Police again raid Lincoln Park.

AUGUST 28
The Battle of Michigan Avenue takes place. The Democrats vote to continue the war. Vice-President Hubert Humphrey is nominated to run for president.

NOVEMBER 4
Republican candidate Richard Nixon is elected president.

APRIL 7
Civil rights leader Martin Luther King is assassinated in Memphis.

JUNE 5
Democratic presidential candidate Senator Robert Kennedy is shot by an assassin in Los Angeles and dies twenty-four hours later.

AUGUST 17
Thousands of activists begin arriving in Chicago, to hold demonstrations during the convention.

To Find Out More

BOOKS

Feinstein, Stephen. *The 1960s From the Vietnam War to Flower Power*. Enslow Publishers, Inc., 2000

Kronenwetter, Michael. *America in the 1960's*. Lucent Books, 1998

McCormick, Anita Louise. *The Vietnam Antiwar Movement in American History*. Enslow Publishers, Inc., 2000

Schuman, Michael A. *Lyndon B. Johnson*. Enslow Publishers, Inc., 1998

Warren, James. *A Cold War: The American Crusade Against the Soviet Union and World Communism*. Lothrap, Lee, & Shepard, 1996

ONLINE SITES

The Whole World Was Watching: An Oral History of 1968
http://www.stgbrown.edu/projects/1968/

The Vietnam War
http://www.vietnampix.com/index.html

Index

About the Author

Tom McGowen is an author of more than 60 books for young readers, fiction and non-fiction. He lived in Chicago and worked in downtown Chicago when the 1968 Democratic convention was held there, witnessing many of the events that took place. His most recent book in the Cornerstones of Freedom Series was *The Alamo*. He is a recipient of the Children's Reading Round Table Annual Award for Outstanding Contributions to the Field of Children's Literature.